FROM GUNK TO GLOW

or

The Gentle Art of Refinishing
Antiques and Other Furniture

by George Grotz
THE FURNITURE DOCTOR

The
Pequot
Press

Chester, Connecticut 06412

1st Printing—March 1952
2nd Printing—June 1952
3rd Printing—September 1952
4th Printing—December 1952
5th Printing—March 1953
6th Printing—June 1953
7th Printing—January 1954
8th Printing—November 1955
9th Printing—May 1957
10th Printing—June 1958
11th Printing—January 1959
12th Printing—October 1959
13th Printing—June 1960
14th Printing—April 1961
15th Printing—November 1961

16th Printing—July 1962
17th Printing—January 1963
18th Printing—September 1963
19th Printing—March 1964
20th Printing—February 1965
21st Printing—November 1965
22nd Printing—February 1966
23rd Printing—October 1966
24th Printing—May 1967
25th Printing—December 1967
26th Printing—June 1968
27th Printing—March 1971
28th Printing—June 1972
29th Printing—June 1973
30th Printing—January 1974

31st Printing—October 1975
32nd Printing—July 1976

PREFACE (With An Ulterior Motive)
TO THE TWENTY-EIGHTH PRINTING

WRITING a book is like walking out onto your front porch in the middle of a dark, starless night, and starting to make a speech. You know you're talking all right, but the question is, is anybody listening?

Well, that's the way I felt when I wrote this book. And I guess it's the most important thing that ever happened to me — that it turned out somebody was listening, after all.

The first thing that happened was that I started getting letters from people, asking me questions about refinishing, and wanting to know where they could buy the different materials I mention using. Then people started coming around wanting to buy my supplies off my shelves.

Pretty soon, I was selling more than I was using. So my wife said, "George, you ought to open a store on the side." The only trouble was that pretty soon the refinishing was on the side of the store — instead of the store being on the side of the refinishing, if you see what I mean?

What I mean is, pretty soon I didn't get to do much refinishing any more, because I was tending the store all the time. And in the end, I lost the refinishing side, which is what the store was supposed to be on the side of in the first place. So to get rid of this thing, you might just say I changed sides.

But to tell the truth — and it's about time — the only reason for this introdution is that my publisher called us and said we had a couple of blank pages to fill up in this edition.

So I guess this is the place to thank all the fine people around here who have helped us get started. What else are you going to do in an introduction to a new edition to fill a couple of blank pages? Can you talk about how writing a book is like going out in the middle of the night and making a speech on your stoop? That's a lot of mush. In fact, it's looney. If anybody heard me they'd lock me up.

But while I think of it, thanks, too, to you people who have bought this book. It's downright gratifying.

—GEORGE GROTZ

I**F** *a man bakes bread with in-difference, he bakes a bitter loaf that feeds but half his hunger.*

—KAHLIL GIBRAN

CONTENTS

THAT NASTY WORD: LYE

Oops, no furniture!

E VERY time the word lye is mentioned, eyebrows are
raised all over the place and one of two stories is
immediately related.

The first is that one of the eyebrow lifters once had a
great aunt who used lye to take paint off a rocker. (It's
never a chair, but always the same rocker.) It took the
paint off all right, but she left a little puddle of lye in the
seat while she ran down to the corner saloon for a beer.
And for Heaven's sake, do you know that when she got
back that nasty old lye had eaten a great big hole right into
the seat and she's had to keep a cushion on it ever since!

And the second mysterious traveler story involves a
great uncle, Cyrus. This kindly old gentleman once refinished a sideboard. Nope, no holes. But some of that
nasty old lye hid in the wood and six months later the finish
he had put on just fell right off.

Of course, both these stories are anxiety manifesta-
tions due to a deep-seated neurosis stemming from childhood
frustrations. The next steps for the tellers of such tales
is to stop driving automobiles because they can kill nice
little old ladies.

Of course, lye is strong. But that's why it removes
four or five layers of paint so much quicker and easier than
paint remover does. And it's no more dangerous than an
automobile, if you know what you're doing and exercise
ordinary care in doing it.

Here is my schedule for using lye — and if you don't think it's the answer to a maiden's prayer, you don't know what you're missing.

1. A good solution of lye is one can (about 17 cents) to 2 quarts of water. Maybe less, but not more water. Believe me. A weaker solution takes too long to soften the paint and that gives it a chance to get in the wood. Apply with a rag wired to the end of a stick.

2. After the lye has softened the paint — five to ten minutes — scrape the bulk of it off with a scraper or old knife. Then scrub the rest off with a stiff brush, using plenty of water. The best way is to do the job outside and use a garden hose. If you've got good pressure, you won't even need to do much scrubbing.

3. Wipe the washed piece dry with a rag and paint it with vinegar. (Soak it on.) Let the piece dry and then paint it with vinegar again. The vinegar neutralizes the lye. To knock the metaphor around once again, it's like having brakes on an automobile.

4. Lye invariably darkens wood. This may be just the rich brown you want. If not, Clorox will bleach the brown out as quickly as you rub it on with a rag. (Don't use a brush — oops, no bristles!)

5. When done there will be a slight fuzz on the wood. With a soft wood this will be quite noticeable. Rub this off with steel wool and you are ready to finish.

6. Lye must be used quickly. In fact, I once had an aunt who left some standing in the seat of a rocker, and before she knew what happened . . .

USE YOUR IMAGINATION

MANY seemingly useless or grotesque pieces of old furniture can be made worthwhile and sometimes extraordinary by physically modifying them. The classic example of this is the marble-topped parlor table. Twenty years ago these were considered junk, and an antique dealer wouldn't give you two dollars for one. But then some unsung genius got the idea of cutting them down to make them into cocktail and coffee tables. And the result is that they now run about $45 in antique shops.

This is a job that is easy for anyone who is at all handy with tools. After lifting the marble off, you will see the frame it rests on is screwed down into the legs or base. What you do is simply saw the top of the base off and screw the frame down to it again.

This cutting down principle can also be applied to cutting the legs off an old fashioned high chest to modernize it. Or for that matter you can cut the bottom drawer off it, though this means putting back on a new base.

Combining pieces is common practice in the antique field. Breadboards and wooden bowls are always finding old legs to stand on. And I was once in the house of an artist who had taken a flush door, and by mounting it on two wooden boxes achieved a stunning table.

Peter Hunt's specialty back when I worked for him was to buy vanloads of old Victorian pieces from the Salvation Army. Then he — or at least slaves like I was — would simplify them by unscrewing and cutting off the gee-gaws and carvings that so fascinated our ancestors at one time. Then he would paint them white with tendrils of ivy climbing up their legs and spreading out across their front, or decorate them in the peasant style for which he was famous.

A fabulous piece is a chair made from an old wooden barrel, though I will admit these are getting harder to find. The idea is to look at what you have, and figure out how it could be modified. Or to decide what you want, go around to the used furniture stores and see what you can find for a few dollars.

If you have a rickety old chest of drawers, why not paint it a flat red toned down with about ten per cent dark gray and give it a set of reproduction antique brasses where the knobs were. Presto, you have an almost genuine Early American chest of drawers. For this sort of thing, buy a wood rasp and go over all sharp edges, hitting the top especially hard. And then sand smooth before painting. Gives it that aged look. Waxing right over the paint will give the piece a different but just as authentic look. What you are imitating, of course, is the paint that Yankee farmers used to make by mixing blood and milk around slaughtering time.

Finding new uses for things is another approach. An old-fashioned life top commode, for instance, makes a wonderful bar or cabinet for a record player and such. The speaker goes underneath where the "thunder mug" used to be kept.

And I suppose everybody has made a girl's dressing table by putting a board across two up-ended orange crates and surrounding it with a frilly skirt — so we won't even mention that!

Lately buggy seats have become a hot decorator's item, selling for as high as $85 mounted on boxes and recovered with bright colored materials.

Nail kegs can be cushioned on top and used for television seats. An old wooden icebox painted white and decorated madly goes well in a playroom. Old picture frames with mirrors put in them make charming coffee tables mounted on legs or simple boxes. Old wash stands cry out loud to be made into flower tables. Commodes and closed wash stands make fine sewing tables.

Now just let your imagination go! You're cornered now. You've no excuses left. Do something!

AN EASY WAY TO REMOVE OLD FINISHES

ANYBODY who has ever tried it knows that the hardest part of refinishing a piece of furniture is removing the old finish. In fact, almost every attic has its chair or table that poor old Aunt Matilda started taking-down but never finished. But taking down does not have to be the messy, discouraging job it usually is — not if you understand the materials you are working with and know a few tricks of the trade.

One of these tricks is the use of wood alcohol and steel wool to remove clear or "varnish" finishes. This works because wood alcohol is a solvent for shellac and most varnish is shellac. Or, to put it another way, very little varnish really is.

(If you confuse easily, stop now. It gets worse from here on.)

But seriously, the explanation is that varnish, as we know it, is a comparatively recent invention. It didn't come into use until about 40 years ago. Before that, shellac was known as varnish. Technically, shellac still is a varnish — one of the "spirit varnish" family of resins that are dissolved in alcohol.

But what is now popularly called varnish is dissolved in linseed oil and thinned with turpentine. As a result, it dries much harder and cannot be re-dissolved with either its "base" (which is the oil) or its thinner, turps.

And there is the key. For shellac can be re-dissolved with alcohol. And because shellac — and other spirit varnishes — were all they had in the old days, the finish on the great majority of antiques can be removed with wood alcohol or any of the shellac solvents sold in hardware stores.

In case you'd like to try it, it takes about a quart of alcohol to do a chair. And while this is not any cheaper than paint remover, it is a lot easier, quicker and cleaner. The technique is this: Pour about a cup of the alcohol in a bowl. Dip into this a small piece of steel wool and, mopping the alcohol on freely, simply scrub the finish off the chair. If you have any lacquer thinner around, add a little of it to the alcohol for even better results.

Work quickly and do only a section of the chair at a time — a leg, an arm, a cross-piece, and so on. The point in working quickly is that alcohol evaporates rapidly. At the right moment, the finish will come off as easily as if it had just been applied. But if you wait too long, the finish will gum up and be hard to remove. When this happens simply apply more alcohol.

When all but a few traces of the finish have been removed in this way, wipe the whole piece off with a rag dipped in the alcohol. And the result — in less than half the time it takes with paint remover — is a clean chair ready for the new finish — whether it be shellac, varnish, wax or oil.

If you had used paint remover, you would have the additional job of scrubbing the wax out of the pores of the wood with turpentine and cleaning up a sticky mess. You would probably also have to sand out marks made by your scraper and would have to apply a primer coat of shellac to the wood before applying the new finish.

Always use alcohol in a well-ventilated place, or the fumes will give you a headache. In fact, if you fell asleep in a closed room full of the fumes, you could wake up dead.

BLEACHED BLONDS I'VE KNOWN

Pass the Clorox, Mom!

FOR the last twenty years the lighter colored woods — especially fruitwoods — have been coming increasingly popular. And most families are saddled with at least some dark mahogany and walnut from a former era. So there is a wide interest in bleaching these, and the results are almost always terrific.

The first step, of course, is to remove the finish. For this you can use any paint remover you like, but I prefer a mixture of half alcohol and half lacquer thinner. I mix this in a bowl and use it to scrub off the old finish with a pad of fairly rough steel wool. As this mixture evaporates quickly, you do a small area at a time. It's a quick, clean and cheap way.

Removing the finish may lighten the piece considerable. This is because stain is often put into the actual finish as well as the wood because this tends to conceal imperfections in the grain and places where two boards were joined together. So you may want to stop now. If so, all you really have to do is wax the piece. Unless you want a brighter finish, in which case you apply a coat of shellac, rub it down with steel wool (fine) and wax or polish the surface. If it is a table top wax will not stand up, so you will want to apply one or two coats of shellac, and a final thin coat of furniture varnish over these. (Varnish is the only thing that will stand up to hot plates, alcohol, vegetable juices, etc.)

But if the stain is in the wood, the next step is bleach it out with Clorox or one of its competitive products. To do this, put on a pair of rubber gloves and scrub it in with a pad of medium or fine steel wool. The reason for using the steel wool is that any traces of finish remaining on the surface of the wood will block the clorox from getting into the surface of the wood where the stain has penetrated. If the result is now light enough for you, you can finish off the piece as indicated in the above paragraph. You don't have to worry about rinsing the Clorox. Just let the piece dry well before finishing off.

Now we come to the problem of the natural color of the wood. There is always some in both mahogany and walnut and some varieties are still pretty dark even after the stain is out of them. But even this color can be bleached out with professional bleaches. However, these are not commonly available because they are basically hydrochloric acid which is not a pleasant sort of thing to have around a store, or a house for that matter. However, such bleaches are available under a number of trade names — usually in two bottles labeled A and B, or 1 and 2. The second bottle being a neutralizer.

A final suggestion: bleached wood is often limed, if the pores have any size at all. The way this is done is that the wood first receives a coat of shellac to seal it. Then a flat white is wiped into the pores. For the best effect the white is killed with a few drops of burnt umber, as we discuss under "Antique White" on page 51.

(13)

STAINING

The tyranny of the paint and varnish tycoons

STAINING furniture should be an easy job, and it would be if clear wood stains were generally available. However, the paint and varnish companies have decided that we Americans are a bunch of boors who don't like to see the beautiful grains that God locked up for us in the hearts of trees.

As a result, these tycoons of no taste insist on putting an opaque pigment in their stains. Your only defense is to be careful not to stir up the can as they direct you to and use the clear liquid that floats on top. But this is pretty weak in color and only good for the lightest effects. The best thing to do is keep hunting around for a hardware store that carries a clear oil stain, sometimes called "a penetrating oil stain."

This is usually hard, but once you have such a stain there is no problem. You just spread it on, let it sink in for a few seconds and then wipe the surface dry. For lighter shades, you can dilute the stain with turpentine — or a turpentine substitute which is just as good and an awful lot cheaper.

Another kind of stain that is almost universally used commercially is analine dye. This comes in two types — the water-soluble and the alcohol-soluble. Both are dry powders with immense coloring strength. One ounce will stain several pieces.

The water soluble dyes must be applied to raw wood and this creates a problem, because the water raises the grain of the wood and it must then be re-sanded. The alcohol variety does not do this, but even so, it has no advantages over the penetrating oil stains (also non-grain raising) and is even harder to obtain.

The big advantage of the alcohol-soluble analine dyes is that they can be used to color shellac or lacquer and so have the effect of hiding the grain without seeming to. But this is rarely desired in home-refinishing. Besides the varnish stains (varnishes with color in them) will do the same thing and these are readily available. As they give a very inferior finish — compared to a clear finish over stained wood — this is only natural. The bad-taste tycoons of the paint and varnish industry see to it that the hardware stores are always well-stocked with them.

P. S. — Most mahogany furniture is a rich brown, yet you will not be able to find any brown mahogany stain. This color can be obtained by starting out with Maple stain and adding small amounts of Walnut to it until you have just the shade that you want.

You can use the same process to get any shade of Cherry stain that you want. In this case start out with Mahogany and add either plain Maple or your Brown Mahogany mixture. For the lighter shades of Cherry, start out with your Walnut-Maple combination and add a little Mahogany.

With different mixtures of these three strains — Maple, Walnut and Mahogany — you can match virtually any wood color. To lighten the shade of any given color, you simply dilute the stain with turpentine.

SHELLAC IS A SNAP

THERE are three finishes that are commonly used on furniture. Varnish is the most resistant to heat, alcohol and mild acids and salts. Lacquer is used commercially because it can be speedily applied with spray guns and stands up almost as well as varnish. But shellac — the traditional finish of the old cabinet-makers — is still the most widely used by the home refinisher.

This is because shellac is an easy finish to apply and then to polish to any degree of lustre or shine that you desire. To be sure, it has low resistance to heat and none whatever to alcohol, which readily dissolves it. But these disadvantages mean little on practically anything but a table top or other counter used for serving food or drinks. On the other hand, shellac is a hard and elastic finish that will take a lot of wear. And a unique advantage of shellac is the ease with which it can be touched up.

Shellac starts out as a resinous substance deposited by small bugs on the trunks of trees in India. It is melted, purified and shipped to this country in dried flakes — and you can buy it in this form. However, it is easier to buy it already dissolved. It comes in two colors: clear and orange. The clear is about the color and consistency of varnish and is the basic shellac that you want. The orange is used to tint the clear — especially for an antique effect.

The best way to apply shellac is in three or four coats, each coat thinned down with three or more parts of wood alcohol to each part of shellac. By not thinning the shellac so much, it is possible to get by sometimes with only two coats, but this takes practice because it is hard to get shellac to flow on smoothly when it is so thick.

The best practice is to let each coat of shellac that you apply dry at least over night. On warm, dry days, however, and especially in the direct rays of the sun, shellac gets as dry at it ever will in two or three hours. Incidentally extremely humid days are bad for shellacking because the alcohol attracts moisture out of the air and gives a white film to the shellac. When this happens the only thing to do is wash the shellac off with steel wool and alcohol and start all over again — on a dryer day, of course.

Another important part of a good shellac job is smoothing out each coat after it has thoroughly dried. This is called rubbing it down and in the old days was done with some fine abrasive, such as pumice, made into a wet paste with water. You can still do this, of course, but you can get the same effect with a lot less work and mess by using fine steel wool. This comes in many grades, from a rough bunch of wire used for cleaning, to a product that seems as soft as down. The "00" grade is good for rubbing the undercoats, but "000" or finer is usually used for polishing the final coat. Roughly speaking, the coarser the wool, the duller the finish you will get, but "0" (medium grade) is about the roughest I have ever used and this was on specific instructions from a customer who liked her finishes so dull that I would call them dead. Most people prefer the smooth gleam given by "0000" (extra fine).

The final step to a shellac finish is polishing it. Usually wax is applied immediately after the final rubbing. But an even superior depth or clarity can be given to the finish if you first rub the surface with a rag that you have dipped in boiled linseed oil. After you have given the entire piece a brisk rub with the oil, wipe it off thoroughly with dry rags and then apply your wax.

THE TRICKS OF VARNISHING

YES, there is a better way to apply a varnish finish! No longer do you need to worry about dust and six-day drying periods. In fact, with the Furniture Doctor's Entirely Unpatented Method, it can be a pretty simple job and during the summer can be completed in one day.

To this phenomenal feat there are two tricks. The first is to coat the raw wood you wish to finish with a sealer coat of good shellac. And in this case "good" means the kind that costs the most and is packaged by any one of the name brand manufacturers of paints and varnishes.

For application, this shellac should be thinned with two parts of wood alcohol to one part of shellac. After application, let the piece you are working on dry in the direct rays of the sun for two or three hours. The day need not be very dry, but on the other hand, don't pick a humid one.

After the shellac has dried, rub it down with a medium-fine grade of steel wool. Assuming you have done a half-way decent sanding job before going to work on the finish, this will give you a satin-smooth surface.

Onto this you brush a quick-drying synthetic varnish recommended for use on furniture. Under no condition use a spar varnish, a floor varnish, or the so-called "four-hour" varnishes. These are undoubtedly of the excellent hardness and wear resistance that their makers proclaim, but you will notice that even their makers do not recommend them for furniture. For while their large proportion of oil gives them excellent body, it also makes them slow drying and gummy.

A synthetic furniture varnish, on the other hand, will set dust free in as short a time as five minutes. Left in the sun, it will be completely dry in four or five hours. For an antique or satin finish, use a satin or dull varnish.

So in good weather, this finish can be completed in one day and used the next. And for ordinary purposes it is as good a finish as can be bought on the very best factory-produced furniture.

P. S. — The big difficulty in applying a varnish finish is getting it to dry. By the same token, the biggest mistake you can make in varnishing is to apply a second coat before the first has fully hardened. The undercoat will then never get dry and the finish will dent and mar easily.

The way to tell hardness is with your fingernail. Test the finish to see how hard you must press your nail into it to leave a mark. It should be as hard to mark as some fully dried piece that you have also tried the fingernail test on.

Incidentally, when you let any finish dry in the direct rays of the sun there is some danger of the finish blistering. This is caused by the piece not being thoroughly dry before you applied the finish or because you have gotten water in your finish. The blisters are actually little steam bubbles caused by the minutest amounts of moisture. So if you are going to let a piece dry in the sun, let it dry off for fifteen minutes before you apply the finish.

When a blister does occur, it can usually be pressed down with the pad of your thumb or forefinger if you have discovered it before the finish is thoroughly dry. If the blister is already dry, chip it out and touch up the hole with a little of the finish on a small camel's hair brush. Later on you can sand the spot smooth with the surrounding finish—using very fine sandpaper, of course.

LINSEED OIL, MY FOOT

FOR years now I have kept my big mouth shut while I listened to people talk about the glories of a boiled oil finish. But lately I find myself getting pretty cantankerous, and I'm going to tell you what I really think. I think that rubbing oil on a piece of furniture is the world's best way to make it look like something the cat dragged in on a dark, wet night.

In the first place, linseed oil darkens the wood. In the second place, it acts like a magnet to dust and grime, and each coat seals some more into the finish, dulling or concealing the grain. In the third place, hot plates — or even just heavy plates, if left long enough — will leave an impression in it. And in the fourth place, whiskey — which I keep in the house purely for testing purposes, of course — will dissolve it. (Wood alcohol will remove it almost as easily as it removes shellac — which is *supposed* to dissolve in alcohol.)

Just how this dirty idea of finishing furniture with linseed oil got started is hard to say. One source for much of its use is the famous Cornell Bulletin on "Refinishing Furniture." This otherwise excellent booklet sets forth the oil finish as something easy to do. And so it is. All you have to do is rub the oil into the wood about once a month for six months.

But most of its use, I think, goes back to a group of people who are trying to be their own ancestors. (Please don't hate me, Elmer, just think of me as ignorant.) Anyway, these people judge furniture purely by how old it looks. And getting it dirty with linseed oil unquestionably makes it look old.

But they can have it. I'll take shellac or varnish any day. For both are clear and hard. Both let you see right into the wood. Both set free the really thrilling beauty that God locked into the hearts of cherry and maple trees —the world's two most beautiful woods. Made in New England, of course!

A FAKE OIL FINISH

It even smells right

I RECENTLY saw the sweetest fake since the wooden nutmeg. It's a "rubbed oil" finish that looks like the real thing, acts like the real thing, and even smells like it. Yet it can be completed in two days instead of a year of weekly rubbings.

In case you didn't know, a finish of boiled linseed oil is supposed to stand up under hot plates, water and alcohol like nothing else will. (But see preceding chapter.) It also has the dubious advantage of being just what somebody's great-great-grand-daddy did. And this is very important to people who take their ancestors seriously.

But to get back to the subject, the ingredients of this fabulous fake are a lot of fine sandpaper, an equal amount of fine steel wool, some well-thinned furniture varnish and, believe it or not, even a little boiled linseed oil. (Mostly for the smell.)

The first step is to sand the wood as smooth as silk. To do this you have to raise the grain several times—until it won't raise any more. What this means is that after sanding it, you wet the wood with water. This will bring out the grain and after the wood has dried out you sand this off. And you have to repeat this process—probably three times or more—until the grain doesn't rise even under a good soaking.

Of course, it is very important that you use very fine sandpaper—about eight 0. And the best way to use it is wrapped around a small block of perfectly flat wood. Do this, and the surface will be smoother than you ever thought wood could get. And you will have achieved in advance of putting on your finish the smoothness that it takes months to achieve by rubbing the surface with oil. This smoothness is the secret of the oil-finished look.

Then give the surface a coat of varnish thinned with two parts of turpentine to one part varnish. Rub this into the wood as hard as you can with the palms of your hands for about five minutes, and then wipe off the excess with a clean, dry rag.

Let this dry—in the sun for speed—and give the surface another light sanding. Just sort of scuff it gently. Then rub off the dust with fine steel wool (grade "00000") and brush on another thin coat of the varnish. Rub down with steel wool, and apply a third coat in the same way. (These thin coats dry fast—in about four hours.)

Give the final coat a good rubbing with your fine steel wool, and sop the whole thing with linseed oil. Put the oil on the unfinished surfaces too, as this will preserve the wood and prevent warping. Let the oil soak in for fifteen minutes and then rub it off hard with a clean rag.

And there you have it—a quick "linseed-oil finish" that few experts can tell from the real thing. And it will stand up better, too.

REFINISHER'S CABINET: PART I

Removing

THE hardest part of any household job is getting somebody else to do it. And getting a piece of furniture refinished is no exception. But one way to stop the other party from squirming out of it is to have all the necessary materials on hand. So the following is a basic Refinisher's Cabinet — a list of materials that will handle almost any home refinishing job.

Wood alcohol — For removing any clear finish over 40 or 50 years old (i.e. before the use of our modern varnishes and lacquers). Using the alcohol from a bowl, scrub the old finish off with a piece of medium grade steel wool. Wipe surface clean with rags moistened in alcohol. Wood alcohol is also used to thin shellac.

Steel wool — Medium grade for the above operation. Triple 0 or finer for rubbing down coats of shellac or varnish before application of next coat or waxing or oiling.

Paint remover — For removing paint, of course. (Tastes awful.) Use where only one or two light coats of paint are on piece.

Lye — For the daring and hardy. Mix two cans to three quarts of water, heat and use out-of-doors only. For pieces heavily coated with paint. Apply with rag wired to the end of a stick.

Vinegar — After you have scrubbed piece on which lye was used with fresh water, let it drain and then wash with vinegar to neutralize any lye that may remain in the pores of the wood.

Oxalic acid — Actually a mild solution in spite of its frightening name, this is used to take out black spots (water marks) that are often found on table tops. May be applied with brush. Mix two ounces of the crystal powder to each quart of water and apply almost boiling.

Clorox — Oxalic acid for water marks and Clorox for the rest. This is the best all-around stain remover and bleach. Apply full strength with a rag as it will destroy the bristles of most brushes.

Wood Fillers — Plastic wood is the best wood filler generally available. But as it does not take stains it must be used in colors. These can be mixed to get an exact match. (See chapter on "Staining" for mixing colors.)

Garnet paper — This is the pale orange sandpaper. Costs more than regular sandpaper but is worth the difference. A smooth wood surface is the secret to a smooth final finish.

Paint scraper — For scraping paint, of course, but a good sharp one can also be used effectively on wood to make the sanding job a lot easier.

REFINISHER'S CABINET: PART II

Finishing

REFINISHING furniture breaks down into two operations — taking off and putting back on. The chapter before this lists the supplies used for removing the old finish. Now let's run through the basic materials used in applying a new finish . . .

Shellac — This by-product of an Indian bug is the commonest of all finishes on antiques. It is also used as an undercoat or "primer" under varnish. Shellac comes either clear or orange colored. Most people consider the pure orange to be too strong when used alone and use small amounts of it mixed into the clear. The proportion depends on your own preference.

Wood Alcohol — Now sold under various trade names, wood alcohol is used as a thinner for shellac. Depending on the number of coats you apply, the ratio of wood alcohol to shellac will range from 50-50 to 5 parts of alcohol to 1 part shellac. About 2 to 1 is a good basic mixture.

Clear varnish — I recommend that a synthetic varnish be used because of its superior drying qualities. This is especially important in cold weather when the natural varnishes are capable of staying tacky all winter.

Dull varnish — This is used as a final coat over one or two coats of clear varnish to give a mellow hand-rubbed effect. After this has dried, a light rub with fine steel wool is all that is needed before waxing.

Turpentine — This is used as thinner for varnish. But it is usually preferable to heat the varnish to make it flow easier. This speeds up the drying. There are many turpentine substitutes on the market selling for about a third of the price of the real thing. Funny thing is, they're all just as good or better than the real thing, too.

Steel wool — This is used for rubbing down a finish to give it a sheen — as opposed to a glossy shine. Grades 000 to 00000 are recommended for this purpose.

Pumice — Traditionalists insist that pumice (and its even finer brother, rottenstone) is the correct material to use for rubbing down. It is made into a paste with water. I doubt, however, that anyone can tell the difference between a rubbing done with pumice and one done with 00000 steel wool.

Boiled Linseed Oil — Not really boiled at all, this is simply raw linseed oil with a dryer added. It is often used instead of wax on a shellac finish. Gives a nice dull glow. People who put a low value on their own time also use it as a finish. Rubbing it into raw wood. To do it right this takes about ten applications, each carefully wiped off, over a period of a year. The result is a grimy look which is for some reason highly prized in some quarters.

And that's it. Of course, by this time you are broke, but look at that happy smile on the face of the man in the hardware store!

RUBBING DOWN

Steel Wool vs. Pumice

I THINK I have more than a passing respect for the early craftsmen who created the antiques that most of us value so highly today. For they so obviously believed that if a thing was worth doing, it was worth doing right. Not just for money, but for self-satisfaction of doing a thing well. But I think it is going a little too far when you insist on using the same methods to restore antiques that were used in creating them.

I am thinking especially of the process of "rubbing-down" or polishing a newly applied finish. For this process the old-timers used pumice in water, followed by rotten-stone in oil — both used in the presence of a lot of elbow grease. But I'll be darned if they wouldn't have used 000 steel wool if it had been available in those days. Nor do I think that anyone could tell the difference between a finish rubbed the old way and one done with fine steel wool.

For the main thing to watch if you want a smooth finish isn't the rubbing-down. The important point is to sand your wood perfectly smooth before applying the finish. And the trick to this is called "raising the grain."

After you have sanded the surface to what seems to be perfect smoothness, wet it with water. This will usually bring out a grain. Then after the wood has dried, sand it smooth again and the surface will stay smooth when you apply your finish.

For a really fine reproduction of an antique finish try this: Mix up one part clear shellac, one part orange shellac and four parts of wood alcohol. Apply four or five coats, or enough to build up an adequate body to the finish. Allow 24 hours drying time between each coat, and rub each coat smooth with 000 or finer steel wool. Rub the final coat with boiled linseed oil and then wipe it off as hard as you can with a dry rag.

This finish will have that "antique patina." And if you want to wax it, it will give you a satin mirror.

FAKING THE GRAIN

Or, silk purses from sows' ears

I THINK the most remarkable wood native to New England is the Tulip Poplar. Frequently known as Whitewood and sometimes called Tulip for short, this wood is a first cousin to the Gumwood that grows in our southern states. And they both have the same chameleon ability to imitate other woods.

I have seen a beautiful cherry table — brought to me by an experienced dealer — turn out to be Whitewood as soon as it was touched by a sander or scraper. And properly "faked," Whitewood will make a perfect Mahogany. As well as a pretty passable Birch, Walnut, Cedar, Hazel and even straight-grained Maple.

The reason for this is that it is a fine and even-grained wood that takes stains well-nigh perfectly. But people who have bought a rare old Cherry table only to find that it is Whitewood are not apt to get rapturous over its deceptive qualities. They are much more interested in knowing how to fake it back to whatever it was supposed to be. This is usually worth doing, because a complete fake is rare. Whitewood is most usually snuck in as a panel in a commode door or as the side of a chest of drawers.

And here is the place where the pigmented stains come into their own. The clear stains will color the wood, but they do not quite do the trick. Besides coloring the wood, you want to obscure the grain. So a simple formula is to use clear stain on the authentic wood, where you want to bring out the beauty of the grain, and used a pigmented stain on the Whitewood, where you want to obscure the grain.

But to obtain an even better fake — the kind that will sometimes fool even the experts — the process is a little harder, although the principle is the same. What you use is a paste wood filler. This is a product used to fill the pores of open-grained wood (such as oak and mahogany) so that you can apply a smooth finish.

This filler comes both clear (a kind of dirty white) and in colors. And you can color the clear and tint the colored with your clear oil stains. You can also dilute it with turpentine. And the advantage of using this colored filler is that with it you can control the degree of obscurity as well as the color of your stain.

The best way to start out is to put about a quarter of a cup of clear wood filler in a bowl. Dilute this with a little turpentine and stir it into a smooth paste. Then add to it in experimental amounts colored filler, clear stain or pigmented stain.

For application, you should thin this mixture down to about the consistency of thin cream. Then brush it on the wood, let it set a few seconds and then wipe it off with a rag. How much you wipe off will control both the color and the degree of obscurity that you leave on the surface. If you want more of either, apply additional coats and let them set a little longer before wiping. If you get too much on, you can wipe it off with a rag dampened with turpentine.

It's a fussy job, to be sure, but nowhere near as difficult as learning how to apply a good varnish finish. And faking is just about the height of the refinisher's art. Or is it the depth? Anyway, once you've done it, you'll feel that you have reached some kind of a personal height or other.

UN-WARPING MADE EASY

Let nature do it for you

ONE of the toughest jobs for the amateur furniture doctor is warped table leaves. But the only reason for this job being tough is that such a mystery has been made out of it by the old-time cabinet-makers. (This is a short-sighted attitude because it has been shown many times that the more amateurs in any given field, the more work there is for the professionals. It's simply a matter of the public getting interested.)

But to get to the point, there is nothing hard about correcting warps. To begin with, warps occur because one side of a piece of wood has not been protected from moisture in the air as well as the other side has. The side that has been left unprotected — usually the underside of a table leaf —therefore takes in moisture and swells up. This causes the leaf to curl, the top of it to become concave.

Of course, if the wood was new when the one-side finish was applied, the leaf will curl in the opposite direction and hump up as the exposed underside dries out and contracts.

The way to correct a warp, then, is by heat and moisture. Special clamps can be used but they are entirely unnecessary and there is a much easier way.

First, strip the leaf of its finish by soaking fifteen minutes with paint remover. Then wash the gook off with rough steel wool and wood alcohol. Paint remover mixes readily with alcohol and this is the easiest, quickest and cleanest way of doing a usually messy job.

Then take your leaves out on the lawn with a kettle of real hot or boiling water. Pour the water on the concave side of the leaves, soaking them well, and turn the leaves over on the grass. You can if you wish, also pour a few buckets of water on the earth where the leaves are to lie. Thus the concave side, facing down, is kept moist while the humped side is dried out by the sun.

All that is left to do now is to check your boards frequently. Some will straighten out in a few hours. There are two in my back yard as I write this that I put out four hours ago and are almost straight already. But if the warp is bad or the wood particularly hard, it can take several days.

If your leaf has a complex warp — that is, if in addition to a lengthwise curl, two opposite corners also turn up — simply place two rocks (at least twenty pounders) on the high corners as the board lies face down. Such warps may take a couple of tries as you often bend the leaf too far. However, it is easy to correct this and wood is satisfyingly plastic when treated this way.

The final step is to let the whole board dry out for a day in the house to see if the job is permanent — and then finish both sides to prevent the wood from warping again. Just a scaler coat of shellac will keep the leaf straight if you want to put off finishing it for a while. Or a thin coat of varnish will also do the job.

OUT, OUT, WHITE SPOT

Or, there's the rub

THERE are two ways to remove white spots from furniture — by polishing them with fine abrasives or by chemical action. Polishing is the method most widely used because it is the safest and will do the job in almost all cases. This is because white spots rarely penetrate all the way through the finish.

The technique is simple. You merely rub the spot with the abrasive until it has been smoothed off and disappears. The trick is in the choice of abrasive. For a really dull finish use the finest grade of steel wool moistened with oil or furniture polish. Most any oil — or for that matter a paste wax — will do.

For the average dull finish, try an ordinary kitchen scouring powder wet to a creamy consistency with water. For a shiny surface use powdered pumice in water and for the truly glossy surface use rottenstone in water. Both rottenstone and pumice are available in the better hardware stores but a perfect substitute is any one of the automobile cleaners which you use to polish your car before waxing it. These will give your furniture the same fine lustre they give to automobile finishes.

The trouble with removing white spots through chemical action is that if they are too strong or left on too long they will remove the finish entirely. However, ammonia is comparatively safe if used carefully. The best way to use it is to make a small pad of a soft rag and wet it with ammonia. Then wring out the pad as hard as you can and spirit the ammonia across the white spot. In other words, brush the spot quickly and lightly with the pad.

For bad white spots on lacquer finishes, do the same thing with lacquer thinner which is available in well-stocked hardware stores. Incidentally, 90% of commercially produced furniture has a lacquer finish — though it is frequently such a good one that it is hard to distinguish it from varnish. In any event, it is always best to try polishing first and use the chemical methods only when the spot is so deep into the finish that polishing has no effect.

REMOVING CIGARETTE BURNS

French Polishing

IT takes a lot of patience, but few jobs give the satisfaction that you can get from removing a cigarette burn from a table top. The first step is to scrape away all the burned finish and wood. Do the rough work with a sharp knife. A kitchen paring knife is ideal if it has a curved blade. When you have removed all the burned finish and scraped out all the blackened wood, smooth the whole spot with fine sandpeper or steel wool.

This usually leaves a spot of much lighter wood as you have to go through the stain which penetrates only the surface of the wood. Cabinet makers usually use aniline dyes dissolved in alcohol to restore color to this area. These can be mixed to get a perfect match, but you can do the same thing with the oil stains available in hardware and paint stores. These come in all standard colors and can be shaded with each other if necessary.

The final step is a useful little trick known as "french polishing." This takes a little practice to get the "feel" of it, but you can practice on any piece of wood you have around and after a few tries you should be able to manage it.

The way it is done is this: Make a small pad of cheesecloth or bandage gauze about an inch and a half square and using about fifteen or twenty layers of material. Wet with shellac and squeeze out the excess so that your pad is soggy — about half way between soaking and squeezed dry.

Then pull up the four corners of the pad and hold them in your fingers so as to make a rounded surface to your pad. To this apply three or four drops of linseed oil. Then with a brisk motion rub the shellac into the spot. At first do not apply much pressure, but in a few seconds the shellac will have begun to harden and you can rub it with about the pressure you would use in polishing wax. Then repeat the process, working shellac into the spot and around its edges until you have built it up level with the rest of the finish.

If the finish of the piece you are doctoring was a dull finish, this will leave a glossy spot. This can be made to match the rest of the surface by polishing it with fine steel wool dipped in oil for a dull finish, with the cleansing powder or pumice in water, for a medium finish, or with rotten-stone or automobile polish for a high shine.

By this method, you can remove burns so that the man who made your table can't tell the difference. And it is very easy to do a cover-up job that can only be noticed by the closest inspection. Incidentally, if you are not satisfied with your job the first time you do it, the shellac can be removed with a pad moistened with wood alcohol and you can start all over again.

A final word: the only burns that cannot be removed by this method are those that go deep into the wood, say, more than an eighth of an inch, as sometimes happens. A really deep hole cannot be filled with shellac, though the mar can be greatly minimized. Sometimes, however, the top of a smaller table can be turned over and the underside sanded and finished to give you a brand new top.

PIANOS ARE EASY

Why start small?

STRANGELY enough, one of the easiest things to refinish is a piano. Of course there is a lot more of it than there is to a chair or a table — but why piddle around with little messes when you can make a truly historic one.

Just think of it! Almost two quarts of "gunk" will come off the average piano. So just let yourself go. Here's your chance to show the world that you can be just as sloppy as anybody else. The usual schedule is one week to refinish the piano — two weeks to clean up the mess.

But there is no getting around the fact that it's easy. This is because practically every piano that was ever made is either sprayed with lacquer or rubbed with shellac — the shellac being rubbed on with a pad soaked in oil, a process called French Polishing. But in either event, both these finishes are easy to remove.

If the finish is shellac, use wood alcohol. If it is lacquer, wood alcohol will work on the older lacquer finishes. But if the lacquer is not one of the early types, lacquer thinner will do the job. Try the wood alcohol first, as it usually works.

The technique is to pour a cup of the alcohol into a bowl and brush it onto the finish. Let this soak in, and brush another coat on in about three minutes. By the third or fourth coat, the finish will be dissolved into a gooey mess than can be easily lifted off with a broad putty knife.

Then take a small piece of steel wool and dip it into some clean alcohol and scrub the remaining scraps of finish loose and wipe the surface with a rag.

Go through this whole operation on one section at a time and when the whole piano has been cleaned, give it a final wiping with a rag dampened with the wood alcohol. This will pick up any of the white bloom that alcohol leaves when it dries in puddles.

And there you are ready to apply your new finish. Because you haven't used paint remover, there is no danger of any of it lurking in the pores of the wood. And because you haven't used a scraper, you have a perfectly smooth surface without days and days of sanding.

A good finish for such a job is shellac. It is easy to apply and to rub smooth with fine steel wool. And if you want an alcohol-proof finish, apply a coat of varnish directly over two or three coats of shellac. For application, the shellac should be cut with two parts of alcohol to one part of shellac. The varnish should be thinned with an equal amount of turpentine substitute.

And don't forget to save the "gunk" that you remove. It's very useful for . . . hmmm . . . well, there must be some use for it. If you figure one out, let me know because I have two and a half barrels of it.

MIRACLE FINISH RESTORER

OF course, my wife will never let me do it, but I would like to sell "The Furniture Doctor's Miracle Finish Restorer." This product is a sort of cure-all patent medicine for run-down finishes that should be a real money-maker — if you didn't try to sell the same town twice!

The annoying thing about this product is that it is about 50% true. That is to say, it will work on the right kind of scuffed and dried out finish. But even then it does take some elbow grease which is quite out of character for a panacea.

On the other hand, this "secret formula" has been widely used by cabinet makers and museum curators for hundreds of years as a finish restorer. And my wife, which is much more important, swears by it. She uses it twice a year on her furniture — all three pieces.

Anyway, you might like to try it. The formula consists of equal parts of boiled linseed oil and turpentine. Yes, that's all, but when it works, it works fine.

The technique is to clean the piece thoroughly with warm soap and water — using steel wool to rub off caked dirt or paint marks where necessary. After the piece has dried thoroughly, rub the formula on with a soft rag. Rub it in good. Then sop on some more of the oil and let it soak in for an hour. Take another soft rag and wipe the surface completely dry. You can then apply a paste wax immediately in the usual method.

The times this formula works the best are when the finish is mainly dried out. On something that has been standing in an attic for 15 or 50 years, it really works wonders.

It's surprising what that soap and water does, too! But if you don't rub oil into a finish after washing it, it will be progressively drier through the years and finally, I suppose, just powder off.

Anyway, what have you got to lose — except your furniture?

STICK TO GLUE

MY wife has a personal approach to the subject of glueing. If I know so much about it, she says, how come she's ashamed to have people in to dinner because her dining room chairs wobble so much. My only answer to that is: if shoemakers' children must go barefoot, so must cabinet makers' wives have wobbly chairs.

But family disputes aside, glueing is the basis of furniture repairing. Not screws, not nails, but GLUE. How often have I grumbled in my figurative beard as I worked on a chair in my shop and found that someone had tried to steady it with nails or screws. A headless finishing nail goes in fine, but just try getting one out without gouging out a half inch of wood so you can get at it with pliers. Screws come out easily enough, but they usually split the wood and always chew up the dowel that they were directed at. But the main objection to screws and nails is that they don't work. Furniture just isn't made that way.

Nor can you glue a chair permanently without taking the loose joint or joints completely apart and cleaning them thoroughly. One reason is this: different kinds of glue (if one of them is dry) will not stick to each other. And then if you have the same kind of glue, it will not dissolve the old glue and mix with it.

Another reason is that butt joints (the flat surfaces of the pieces where they come together) have little holding power. It's the dowel that does the holding. That's why it's there.

The usual way to clean a joint is to scrape it with a sharp edge. A knife will do, but you'll find a half-inch chisel much easier to handle and work with. And if there is a lot of glue, hot vinegar will help by dissolving it.

After the joint is clean, you may find that it is now loose. The trick here is to tear narrow strips of cloth and place them across the end and down the sides of the dowel. Soak both sides of them with glue. Also put plenty of glue into the hole.

The last step is to put the joint together and let it set under pressure. Now don't make believe you didn't see that sentence. No tickee, no shirtee — no pressure, no hold. People who think that they can glue joints without pressure are what keep cabinet makers in business. You see, it's easy for them to apply pressure, because they have pipe clamps (adjustable to any length). But you can do almost as well — good enough for the average job — by using clothes line or rope.

Tie the joint just a trifle loosely with a loop of the rope — and then put a stick through the loop and twist it just as tight as you can. It's the old principle of the tourniquet.

Get it clean, get it tight, and it will stay stuck.

RESTORING OIL PAINTINGS

It's all on the surface

THE restoration of old paintings is a fine art in its own right and usually involves the repainting of torn and flaked areas. In fact, some restorers have even accomplished the feat of taking the paint off of one canvas and putting it on a new one. As one handbook on the subject says, this requires "considerable skill." No doubt!

However, the cleaning of an old painting — which is 90% of a restorer's work — can be done by an amateur with results that are usually remarkable. And you don't have to worry about ruining a possibly valuable piece of property if you just follow two simple rules: (1) Before using it on the main body of the picture, test your cleaner (see below) on some unimportant section at the edge of the picture, (2) Clean a small patch at a time. This way, if anything goes wrong you can stop it without having done much damage. Then if the picture is worth it to you, you can still take it to a professional restorer.

But it's really fairly simple once you understand the structure of an oil painting. With rare exceptions, they are made up of four layers. The first is the canvas. Second is a coating of "gesso," applied directly to the canvas. This is a sort of white paste or glue which adheres well to the canvas and forms a base for the oil colors themselves — which are the third layer.

The fourth and top layer is a transparent varnish. And it is this last layer that interests us most. For it is on and into this protective coating of "varnish" that the dirt gets.

By removing this coating we can restore the painting to its original color and depth.

But getting down to cases, the following is the basic working schedule:

1. Take the canvas out of its frame and wash it gently with turpentine and a soft cloth. Never use water. It will seep through minute cracks in the oil colors and soften the gesso base. This will cause the cracks to enlarge and the oil to flake off.

2. For a safe cleaning solution, start out with a mixture of half turpentine and half wood alcohol. If this doesn't work, gradually increase the proportion of alcohol until you are using it full strength. If this doesn't work you will have to get the ethel acetate or acetone. These can be had from wholesale paint dealers and art supply houses. These, too, you start out by using with turpentine and gradually increase their proportion.

3. To apply the cleaner, use little wads of cotton, discarding them as each gets dirty. Don't rub hard or you will rub off some of the oil colors. Instead, keep your stroke gentle, but increase the strength of your solution until you get results. A stronger solution is safer than friction.

4. If the cleaned painting has blooms or even a complete haze of white over it, this will be removed by applying kerosene or thin mineral oil.

5. Wash the cleaned painting with turpentine, dry off with cotton and allow to dry out overnight.

6. Coat the cleaned painting with a fresh covering of shellac. This will be necessary to bring out the colors. Use clear shellac, thinned with four parts of alcohol to each part of shellac. Coat once only.

You are now a restorer of old paintings.

Incidentally, just what this has to do with *"The Furniture Doctor"* is just as big a mystery to me as it is to you.

ART VS. AGE

And a process for manufacturing antiques

THE reason so many people find satisfaction in restoring antiques is that the work is not merely labor, but actually a creative art. For art is a process of elimination, of selection or discrimination whichever of the words you prefer. And a table or chair can be refinished in many different ways for many different effects. As the old saying puts it, "Every man to his taste," said the old lady as she kissed the cow.

Some like their finishes bright, some like them dull. Some like wood dark and some like it light. Some like varnish, some like shellac, some like lacquer. Some like signs of wear and others don't. Some like brass tarnished and some like it bright.

Some like their antiques to look old. Some like them to look like Duncan Phyfe just finished rubbing them down.

But I say, if you are going to restore — really restore. Respect the art of the craftsman who created and developed the work of art that you are lucky enough to possess. To me it is a choice between antiquity and art. And antiquity for antiquity's sake I cannot see.

For one thing, art is a lot harder to come by than antiquity and old things are not necessarily beautiful. But for those who prefer antiquity, I suggest the following recipe:

Take one piece of Grand Rapids maple. Soak in a pond three weeks or leave out one winter. Dry out and sand with coarse sandpaper. Rub with a mixture of turpentine and linseed oil (half and half). Let soak for thirty minutes and wipe dry. Allow to dry for three days more. Apply a wash coat of shellac. Allow to dry one hour. Take the piece out in your back yard and lash fifty times with a set of rusty automobile chains. Rub thoroughly with rich black earth. Clean off with steel wool. Mash the end of one leg by beating it with a hammer. Use a finishing nail to make worm holes, keeping them scattered roughly in one section of the piece. (Or blast at a range of ten feet with two rounds of bird shot). Apply finish coat of shellac and rub down with fine steel wool.

I, of course, have no experience in this sort of work, but I did know a gentleman that made a very good living at it, and it was he that gave me the above recipe.

HOW TO PAINT LIKE A PRO

THE trouble with painting is that it looks so easy that people don't have any respect for the craft of it. They grab a can of paint they haven't mixed thoroughly, stick a brush that isn't really clean into it, and slap the paint on a surface that they haven't scuffed smooth and still has traces of an ancient wax on it. Then for one of 42 possible reasons the job is a mess, and they give up. But if one pays a little attention to what one is doing — and spends an extra 15 minutes on the job — one can produce a job equal to the work that comes out of factories using $50,000 worth of sanding, spraying and drying equipment. So this is what you do:

Prepare the surface: Wax on the surface is the worst thing because you can't see it, and it will cause many paints to never dry or have off-color streaks. And the only thing that will remove wax — short of a blow torch — is turpentine or one of the trade-named paint thinners. So the first step is always to wash down the piece with one of these.

The second step is to sand any rough places with fine sandpaper. Also take the sharpness off of any corners and edges with sandpaper. Now dust the piece thoroughly, and finally wipe it with a tack rag. To make a tack rag, take a piece of cloth about the size of a face cloth. Wet it completely with varnish or the color paint you are going to use. Then squeeze and wring it out as hard as you can. This will pick up dust instead of just moving it around as a dust cloth does.

Now the brush. The only really clean one is a new one. And expensive ones are a snare and a delusion. The smart thing — I think — is to buy cheap two-inch ones and use a new one for each job. This is because the only way to get paint out of a brush is to wash it in about ten rinses of thinner, and then with soap and hot water for five minutes. A varnish brush, of course, is kept wet. That is, it is suspended in a can of thinner by a hook on the handle or a wire through a hole in the handle so that the bristles don't touch the bottom of the can. If you haven't done this to your brushes — or washed them as described — go down in the cellar right now and throw them away.

Next, the paint — or shellac, or varnish. Try always to buy only what you use. This is being pound wise instead of penny foolish. Once exposed to air, all three spoil — shellac in a few months. Stir paint, but don't thin it. Thin varnish about 15% with paint thinner. Thin shellac to 50-50 with alcohol or the so-called shellac solvents, which are really alcohol.

And here is where people begin leaving me: Never put your brush in a can, but work out of a bowl or soup dish. Pour a little into the bowl at a time. This way if you get some dirt on your brush, you won't get it into the can before you notice it, and you can throw away the paint or whatever you have in your bowl, and clean your brush.

Application now becomes a pleasure, and the only hints I can give on this seem obvious. On vertical surfaces work from the top down to avoid curtains. But even more important don't try to put two coats on at once. Take the time to put two thin coats on if this is necessary. In fact, always put on as thin a coat as you can. Take an area about 18 inches square and brush your paint hard onto the surface. Then tip it off with the ends of the bristles, and move on to the next section. In other words, don't try to do too big an area at once, and you won't have to go back, which is a major source of trouble with quick-drying paints and shellac. Varnish, too, if the room is as warm as it should be.

(49)

While the above are basically directions for painting, they all apply to shellac and varnish. In the case of *shellac* it is most important to finish a small area at a time and not go back. When doing a table-top, the trick is to do a narrow strip along one edge (stroke with the grain) and move towards the center and on across to the opposite edge.

With *varnish,* there are several other points to remember. First never use spar varnish, though most clerks in hardware stores will tell you it is the best. Use only a varnish that says on the can that it is for furniture, and definitely not to be used out of doors. The reason spar varnish is no good for furniture is that it contains a lot of oil and very little drier so that it will stand up to sun and rain, hot and cold. So it dries on top, but not underneath. The best of all are the modern plastic varnishes, which dry hard and therefore can be "polished" with fine steel wool before waxing or polishing. And it is this final rub-down with steel wool that gives the satin-smooth glow that factory finishes have. Finally, always apply varnish in a dry and warm room, as it will dry poorly on damp or cold days.

These, then, are the basic rules of applying paint and other finishes. From here on we can talk about special techniques and ideas with the assumption that all of the above applies.

ANTIQUE WHITE

THESE words — antique white — mean many things to many people. Basically, it is done to pieces with a lot of carving or mouldings. And it can range from a chalky white with gold leaf peeking through at the high spots to a semi- gloss without gold and characterized by the dark browns in the crevices of the carvings and mouldings.

The Marie Antoinette effect was achieved by gold leafing the high spots of a piece. Then a flat white containing very little oil was applied to the whole piece. And after this was dry, it was rubbed off the high spots, allowing the gold to show through.

The modern technique is slightly different because we are trying to reproduce an aged look — especially dirt in the crevices — that the originals have been a couple of hundred years acquiring. So our basic approach is to first apply a coat of enamel. This may be white, off white, or pale gray. Off-white, or "killed" white, is the most popular. This means that a few drops of black or burnt umber have been mixed into the paint to kill the brilliance of pure white. You buy the burnt umber in tubes, thin it with paint thinner to paint consistency and add one to three drops to a pint of white enamel.

After this enamel is thoroughly dry, you can steel wool it to dull the surface, though some people prefer to leave it glossy. You now prepare a glaze of raw umber (which is a dead brown) or raw umber (which is yellowish, mustardy brown) or burnt umber which is a rich, dark reddish brown) — or a mixture of two or all of these browns, which are called "earth" colors.

(51)

(Incidentally, when I refer to "colors," I do not mean paints, tubes of pure pigment, ground in oil, which are sold for the purpose of tinting paints.)

Returning to the glaze, this is prepared by pouring half a cup of dull varnish into your bowl. Then with a small brush you mix in about a teaspoonful of the color. Now thin the varnish with about two tablespoons of thinner, and we are ready.

If you are doing a chair, start with a leg. First brush the glaze on, getting it into all the crevices. Now get a small pad of burlap in the glaze, wring it out hard, and wipe the excess glaze off the leg, leaving it in the crevices and streaks of it along the length.

For a different effect, you may use a wiping pad of soft cotton, and leave no streaks along the length of the leg. And if you decide you don't like the color, wash the glaze off with thinner, mix another glaze, and try something else. Many variations are possible — including a darkish green glaze — and it is a matter of your personal preference.

Finally, there is the matter of the gold on the high spots. This isn't usually done any more, because it makes the piece pretty ornate, and few rooms in modern houses are up to this. The only place you see it often is in pictures of interiors in Vogue or Harper's Bazaar. That is for living room furniture. But it is pretty common for frilly boudoirs and powder rooms of those who aren't ritzy enough to get their living rooms in Vogue.

Another way the gold is made to seem to peek through, is to wet a pad with gold paint, or gold bronzing powder mixed into varnish — which is gold paint. This is then brushed lightly over the high spots, and the harder you brush, the more gold seems to be breaking through the white.

And that's it. Don't even wax or polish it for dullest possible effect.

LIMED OAKS FROM LITTLE LEMONS GROW

H ERE is a good example of the importance of fitting the method of decoration to the raw material, because you can only get the limed effect with open-grained wood. Oak, of course, is best. But you can also use walnut and mahogany, even chestnut, when they are the kind that have open pores. With the last three it depends on the angle to the log on which the planks were cut. So sometimes you find open pores, and sometimes you don't.

But assuming you have a large-pored wood, the process of liming is very rewarding for the amount of effort it takes. The first step is to remove some of the present finish, which includes getting the filler out of the pores. So the trick is to let paint remover soak in long enough to penetrate this filler in the holes. Then take the remover off with a stiff brush. You can use a stiff new scrubbing brush, the floor kind, or fine-bristled wire brushes, even a tooth brush for corners and mouldings or carvings. After the remover is off, keep dipping your brush into a bowl of wood alcohol as you work on getting the filler out of the pores.

Now let the piece dry thoroughly, and with fine sandpaper go over the surface to remove any fibers the brushing may have loosened. Then dust off, and wipe with a tack rag.

The paint you now brush on may be of any color you want, but it must be glossy enamel thinned down so that the mixture in your bowl is from 15% to 35% thinner. (You will have to see how it works to get the right consistency.) The idea now is to brush on a thin coat, brushing the paint out well, the point being not to fill the holes with paint.

This is easier than it sounds, as it just sort of happens. When this coat is dry, lightly scuff the surface with sandpaper again, wipe with the tack rag, and apply a second coat.

Now comes the wiping process to fill the pores with a contrasting color. White is usually used, as the base coat is usually black, a dark green or dark gray — though, of course, you can use any color you want and fill the pores with any color you want.

What goes into the pores is, of course, paint, and you can use most anything, even poster paint. But most people prefer flat white, and to get the pores as full as possible, you can pour the top off a small can of flat white before stirring it. But this is unimportant, because you can experiment with different consistencies to see the slightly different effect you get. And if you don't like it, you can wash it off with another rag wet with thinner. Incidentally, the wiping on is done with a piece of cloth about the size of a man's handkerchief folded up into a small pad.

Appearance-wise the piece is now finished. But tops of tables and bureaus really need a protective coat of varnish after the paint in the pores has dried. So you might as well do a good job and go over the whole piece. When this varnish is dry, rub it down with fine steel wool, stroking with the grain, and finally wax or polish.

UNCLE GEORGE & CAESAR

T HE most unforgettable character I ever knew was an uncle of mine whose name I bear. By the time I came onto the scene, Uncle George was a cabinet maker of growing reputation and after his death he assumed somewhat mythical proportions. But this was not due, I am afraid, to the excellence of his work, which w.'s usually pedestrian — if not downright jaywalking.

But Uncle George was a rich character in every sense of the word except money. In his youth he had gone flat broke to California to look for gold, and had returned four years later in debt up to his ears and accompanied by a wife and five children. But the children were his in name only as his wife was the widow of a miner who had started an argument with a gentleman who was about a 10th of a second faster that he was.

But all his trouble never got Uncle George down. In fact, he was incurably optimistic and, in a carefully camouflaged way, almost gay. It was as if he figured things had gotten so bad even worrying wouldn't help them. Or as I often heard him say, after some real fine catastrophe, like spilling a gallon of shellac, "Boy, you look at a man in an enviable position. From where I stand, up is the only direction left to go."

This incident, like all my memories of Uncle George, took place at our old family homestead up in "York State." It was an old run-down farm near Kooksakie (purely phonetic spelling) and not far from Tappan and the High Tor section of the Lower Hudson Valley. It was here that he took his "store-bought" family on his return from California at the age of 35 and with no discernable prospects for the future.

"When I put foot on that land," Uncle George used to tell us during our summer vacations years later, "I knew that I was home at last. Right then and there I resolved to build that farm back to its former glory. In fact, I felt that way for two or three hours."

Or sometimes he would give an alternate version of his spontaneous reaction to farming. "I walked out into the fields," he would say, "and picked up a piece of earth. I crumbled it and let it run through my fingers. But no matter how hard I tried to look at it differently, to me it was still just dirt."

But during his earlier years Uncle George had held many jobs. And once for two or three weeks he had been a cabinet maker's helper. And being my Uncle George, this led him to believe that he was qualified to hang out a shingle as a cabinet-maker. Furthermore, he found a barn full of old furniture on the farm and this looked like the quickest and easiest way of getting some food for the hungry mouths that surrounded him. Repairing or refinishing a piece at a time, he would cart it into town and sell or trade it for the necessities of life. And without actually meaning to, by the time he had worked himself through that barn he had become a fair cabinet-maker and finisher. Besides, the articles he had sold in town had given him something of a local reputation. It was as if he had tricked himself into settling down to a trade and even an established business.

Some men are born to success. Others achieve it. But like Caesar, or somebody, my Uncle George had to have it thrust upon him.

UNCLE GEORGE VS. THE "SUMMER LADIES"

WHEN I was a small boy, my Uncle George was my hero, and I guess he still is. It's not that he amounted to much. He never had any money. And I don't think he ever got around to even thinking about position in life. He wasn't much of a provider for his family. And as a cabinet-maker he was a fine plumber. But he certainly was a character and I guess he couldn't help being what God made him. One of the things he used to say was, "It's hard to judge a man in this life, when even God waits until he's dead."

But to my mind, my Uncle George reached titanic heights one summer when I was 11. In those years, I used to spend the summer vacations at his farm in the Hudson Valley. And it seems to me that I remember everything that happened clearly. But I doubt it. What I probably remember are the hundreds of times the tale has been retold in my family. Certainly the action of my Uncle George could not have the significance to a boy of 11 that they have to me now.

At any rate, I'm sure the incident did occur and came off something like this: One morning Uncle George got a telephone call to come and look at some work for him at one of the big summer mansions overlooking the Hudson. When he arrived, the lady of the house took him to a barn and showed him six small tables, the tops of which had been ruined by glass marks and cigarette burns.

"Do you think you could fix these up for me?" she asked.

"Yes, ma'am," my Uncle George answered.

"Well, how much do you think it will cost?" she went on.

"About five dollars each," drawled Uncle George.

"All right," smiled the lady.

But Uncle George shook his head, "I could do them, ma'am, but I'm not gonna do them."

"Well, for heaven's sake, why not?" asked the incredulous matron.

"Ma'am," said my Uncle George, "there's no point in my getting started with you. With friends like you've got, I'd only have to do them all over again next year."

But there was one time one of the "summer ladies" had it on Uncle George. She was wandering around his shop looking at pieces he was working on when she came to a table he had just finished varnishing. Lightly, she ran her fingers across the top.

Just then Uncle George looked up and saw what she had done. "Good Almighty Lord," he shouted, "don't touch that table. Can't you see it's wet?"

"Oh, that's all right," the summer-lady casually replied, "I still have my gloves on."

UNCLE GEORGE SELLS A DESK

SOME people thought that my Uncle George was what the younger generation now calls "a hydromatic hill-billy" — that is to say, shiftless. However, I don't agree, I think he was one of the great unrecognized philosophers of his time, or of any time for that matter.

The trouble with his life (if you object to ne'er-do-wells) was that he never made a connection. Fame and fortune are accidents. The way he put it was, "For great things to happen, the man and the opportunity must meet." What he meant was: what would have become of Napoleon if he had never been born in a time of peace? Who knows which of us, born in a different time or environment, would make an Emerson, a Rockefeller — or a Stalin?

But that sounds like I am excusing my Uncle George for never getting anywhere. And I'm not. On the contrary, I admire him for the adjustment that he made to life. He tried for many years to be a success according to the standards of the society in which he lived. But I don't think his failure to do so really meant that *he* was a failure. It just means that he didn't meet those standards. And I, for one, do not think the standards of the majority are necessarily the best.

But eventually my Uncle George came to a turning point. He spent two-thirds of his life being a "failure" in a world he did not make. But for the last third of it, he was a success in a private world of his own.

What happened was that he picked up a little book and read one sentence in it. Can that happen? Can such a little thing change the direction of a life? Perhaps not. But I think it can be a trigger that sets off stored-up forces. At any rate, I have the book, and it's a wonderful sentence:

"If a man bakes bread with indifference, he bakes a bitter loaf that feeds but half his hunger."

When he read that sentence, my Uncle George was trying to sell subscriptions to a business encyclopedia. He was probably the worst such salesman in the United States and on the verge, I imagine, of suicide — that one statement nobody can contradict.

Two weeks later he was building furniture with his own hands, and was as close to a completely happy man as I have ever known. You see, for all the scorn the world heaped upon him, my Uncle George was a man of action. And I find it hard to call a man shiftless who can take his life in his own two hands and completely make it over.

But this is getting downright serious, isn't it!

Did I ever tell you about the time my Uncle George tried to sell one of the summer people a desk for $1,000? In those days, such a desk was worth about $100, maybe a little more.

Well, anyway, the summer gentleman laughed at such a price and said, "I'll give you eighty dollars for it."

"Sold," said my Uncle George.

"But why," asked the man, "did you ask a thousand dollars for it when you were willing to sell it for only eighty?"

"Well," said my Uncle George, "I just thought you might like to own a piece of furniture that cost you a thousand dollars."

HOW TO GET SOAP OUT OF A WELL

E VERY Spring we get letters from our city friends — full of the usual hints about how nice it would be to get out into the country for a week-end. Some of the things they do are incredible. Last summer an artist friend of ours dropped a bar of soap down our well.

When he told me about it, I said, "You're kidding." When he just shrugged his shoulders and walked away, I figured he was. So that night he left. Next morning we had more soapy water than anybody in New England. The more buckets we pulled up, the soapier it got. My wife said, "Why don't you forget it and start a laundry?" It was Palmolive. Good soap, but it doesn't float. He might at least have used Ivory.

I finally made a porcupine affair by driving a lot of nails through a board. Then I weighted this down and tied it to a string. I "walked" this porcupine across the bottom of the well a couple of times, and by gosh I got the soap on the first try.

That well is my worst problem out here. When we first came, I had to go down it to clean out the garbage on the bottom. There were two beer cans, a full bottle of Coke, some gears and a lot of wet leaves.

First the local fire department came and pumped it out so I wouldn't drown. When it came time to go down the rope, I got as far as my armpits and found out that I was a coward. But there were my wife and the fire department standing around like waiting vultures. Also, the well was filling up with water again. So down I went. At the time, I really didn't expect to come up alive. But what could I do? It was a choice between a difficult death and an impossible life. If I hadn't gone down, it would have been all over town in five minutes. Of course, we could move, but I'd have to get a new wife, too. And I'm never going through THAT again.

Down on the bottom, I began to feel better. I looked up to see if I could see the stars. But that's a lot of hogwash. At least, I couldn't see much sky either. It looked just like a little round moon of blue.

So there I was shoveling this junk into a bucket and somebody was hauling it up to the world. At one point a piece of rotten leaf got into my mouth, and without thinking, I spit it out. What do you think of that? A guy that would spit in his own well?

Finally they hauled me out, and I went around thinking I was a hero for two weeks. I told people I wasn't scared at all. Then I read in the paper about this young fellow cleaning his well up in Litchfield, and it caved in on him. He was just my age, and it sure gave me the shakes.

Well, I proved I can do it if I have to, so next time I'll pass the buck to somebody else. Maybe I will invite that artist up for another week-end — and then goad him into going down it. Him and his Palmolive. It'd serve him right if it did cave in on him.

AUCTION FEVER

Or, Terror in the Afternoon

I'M disappointed in that little boy of mine. When he arrived eighteen months ago, I was full of hope. Now there, I said to myself, is a kid that will amount to something. But he just doesn't have any spirit. I took him to the "5 & 10" last Saturday and he didn't steal a thing.

Incredible! When I was a boy, it was considered mentally deficient not to come out with your pants stuffed full. The worst part of it was that I explained to the girl who ran the place that I would pay for whatever he took. And then he didn't take anything. It was humiliating.

But maybe there is some hope for him. This morning he has a hangover. He's only been up a half hour and he's walking around yawning, sucking on his blanket and complaining about everything. I'm not surprised. We took him to a party last night and he passed out on the couch, at nine-thirty.

As a matter of fact we've had trouble with that boy since he was three months old. One day last summer we took him to an auction down in Old Saybrook.

It was a good auction, too. Mickey Ellis ran it, and Red McNicholas was helping him. The only trouble was that a little baby like that requires constant attention. So we had to take turns looking at the auction. And when he got hungry it somehow turned out that it was my turn to take care of him.

His mother dug out a jar of some kind of pulverized vegetables, and I tried to feed him. The first three spoonfuls went fine. But then he decided he wanted to hold the spoon himself. What a mess!

Pretty soon it occurred to me that a bib would help. He was beginning to look like the Thing From Another Planet. So I reached up and tapped my wife in the middle of the back and said, "Have you got a bib?"

"A bib!" I shouted with some excitement as the baby had his left hand in the vegetable jar.

"Twenty-five cents!" called my wife to the auctioneer.

"Bib, bib," I shouted to her.

"Fifty cents," shouted my wife.

And so it went for about thirty seconds. Of course, that's not a long time, but things move pretty fast at an auction. And by the time my wife and I got straightened out she had gone to $3.75 and we were the proud owners of a cardboard box containing two broken plates, four cups without handles, and one second-hand corset.

I might add that the reason the price got so high was that my wife was bidding against herself. Every time Mickey got ready to say "Sold," I would tap my wife on the back and shout "Bib" at her. And she in turn would raise herself another twenty-five cents.

And by the third or fourth time this had happened people began to notice my wife's frantic attitude. So they joined in. They figured that if my wife wanted that box so badly, maybe they did too.

Poor Mickey! Every time he'd take a bid, he'd look down into the box to see if he hadn't missed something. When I finally got up to see if I could put a muzzle on my wife, I caught a glimpse of him. He was looking out at the audience with half a pleased smile on his lips, but there was terror in his eyes. He looked as if he thought the world had gone crazy — and he didn't know whether he should stay and take their money or grab his cash box and run.

Finally, when my wife shouted three seventy-five, he shouted back "Sold!" — without letting her or anybody bid again. I guess he figured she wanted that corset too much not to get it.

So you can see why I don't think that boy of ours will ever amount to much. He's been a trouble-maker from the start.